Hot Cross Buns

Part 1

Part 2

Part 3

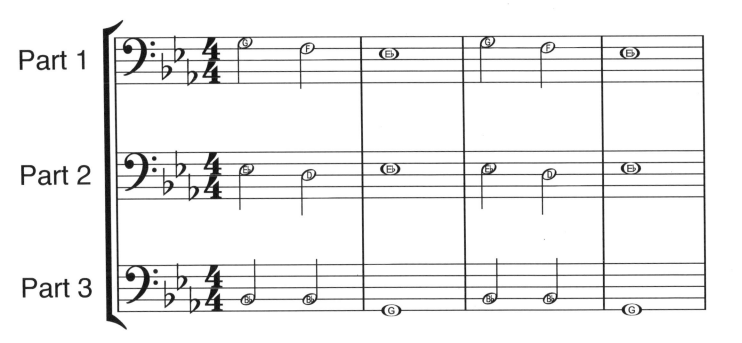

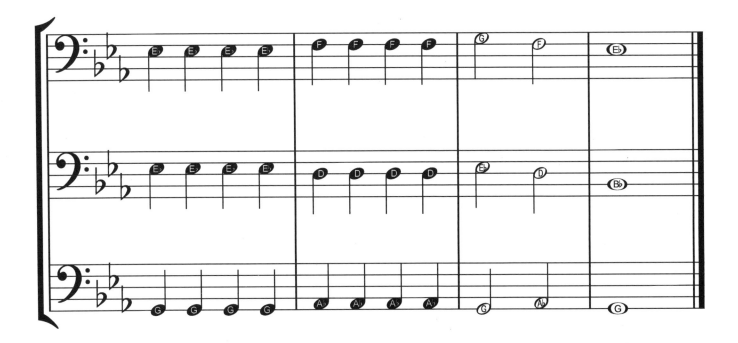

Mary Had a Little Lamb

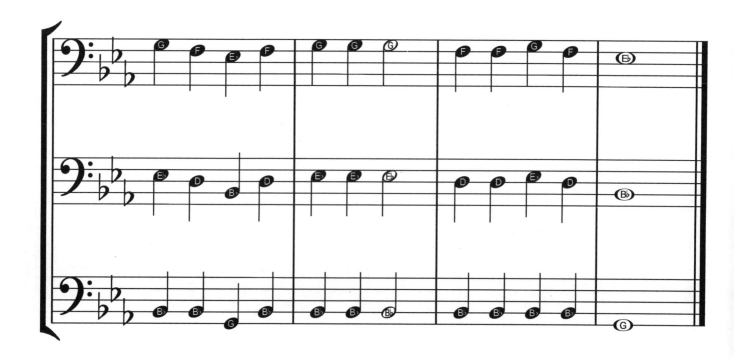

Au Claire de la Lune

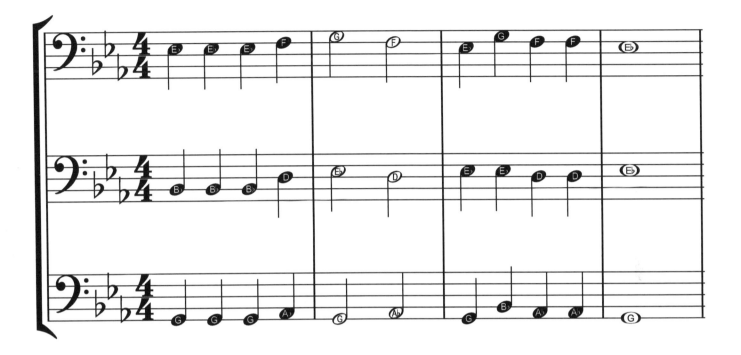

Good King Wenceslas

Love somebody

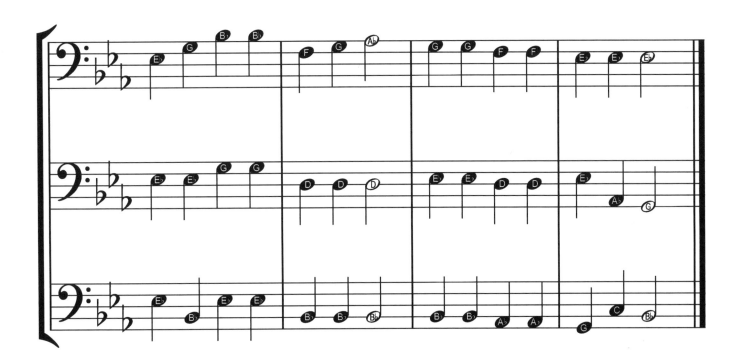

Oats & Beans & Barley Grow

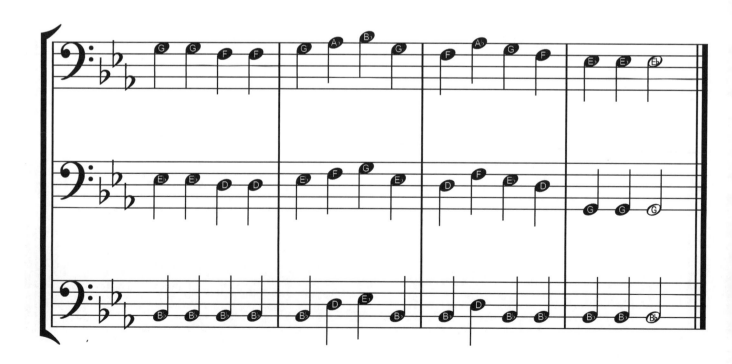

Lightly Row

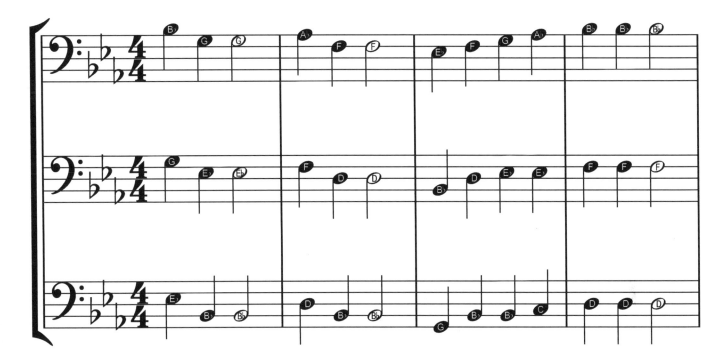

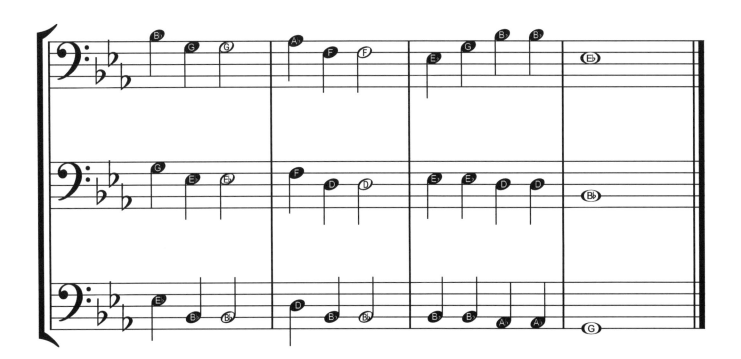

Aura Lee

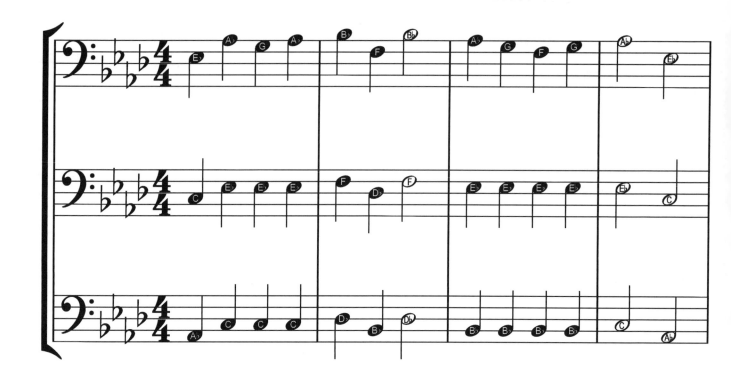

Go Tell Aunt Rhody

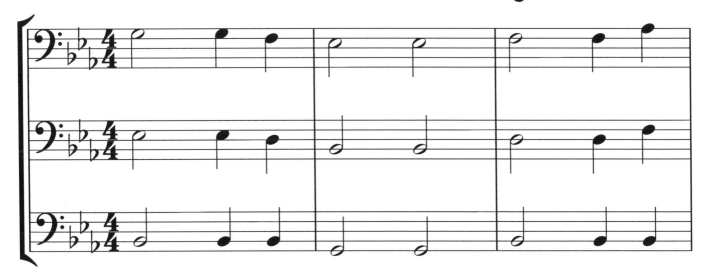

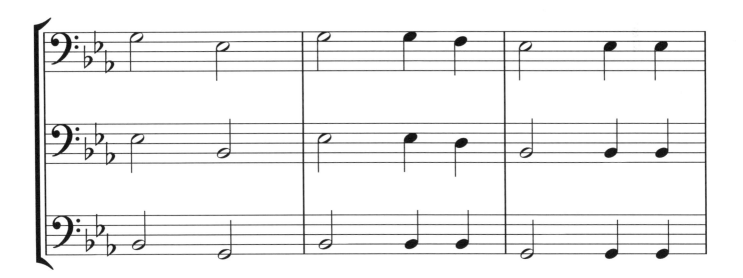

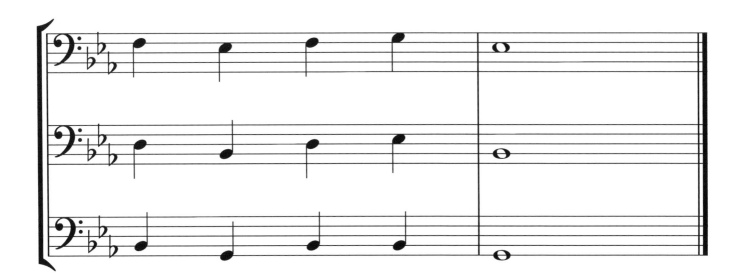

Frog song

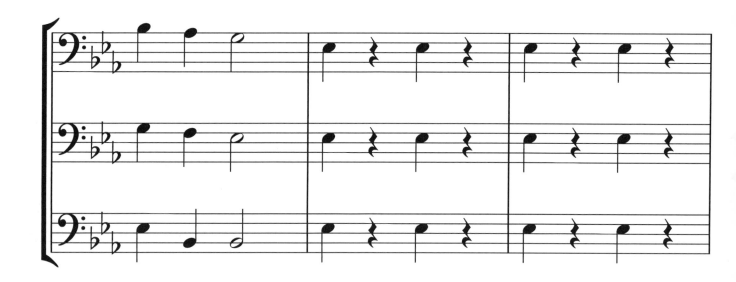

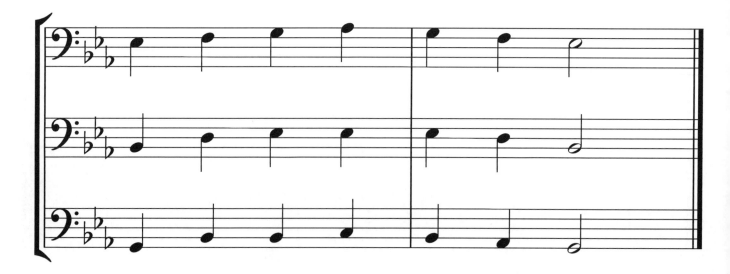

Alouette

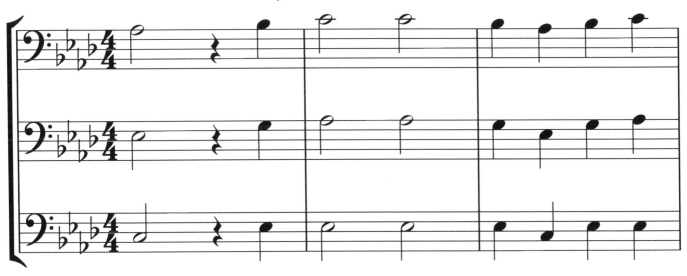

Camptown Races

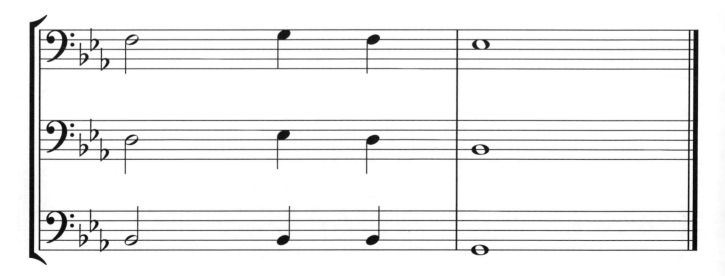

London Bridge

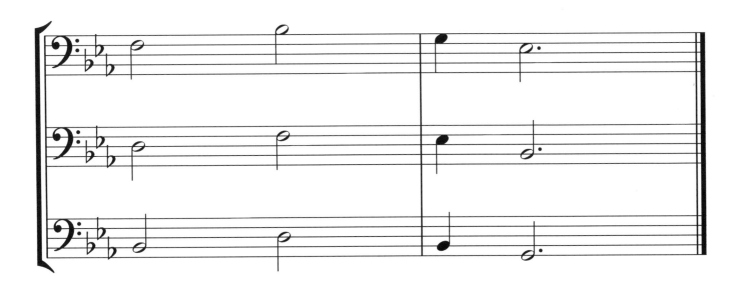

saints Go Marchin' In

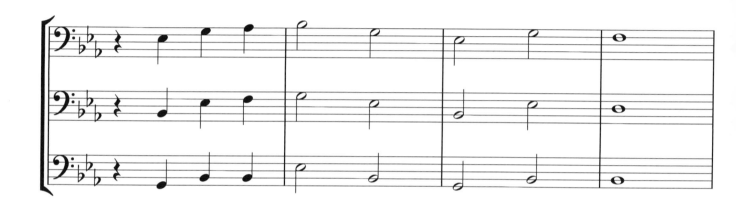

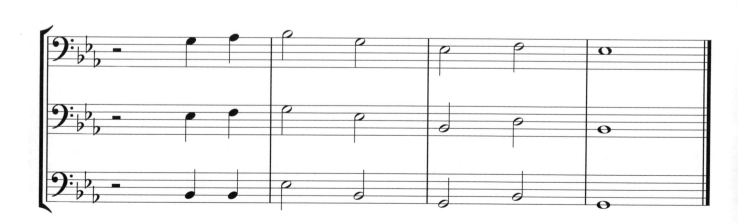

Long, Long Ago

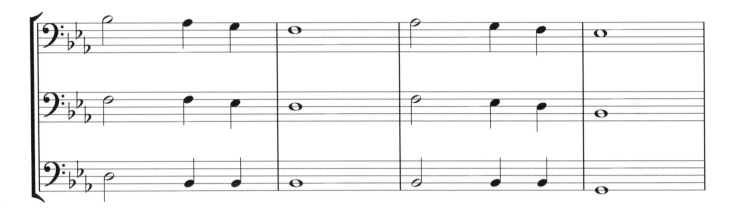

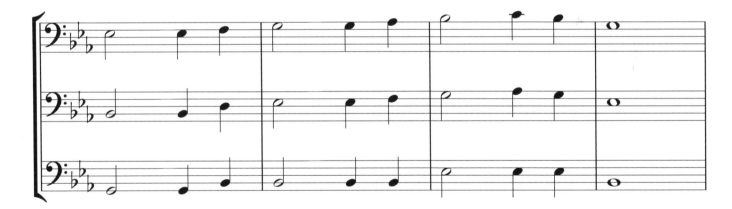

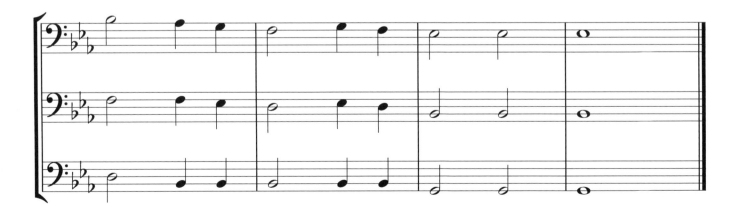

Rondo alla Turca

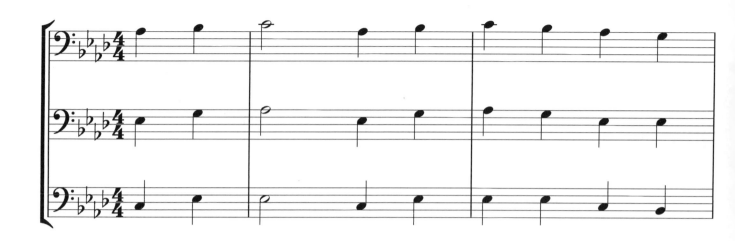

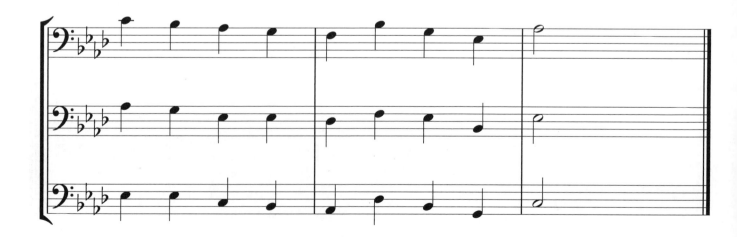

Down by the station

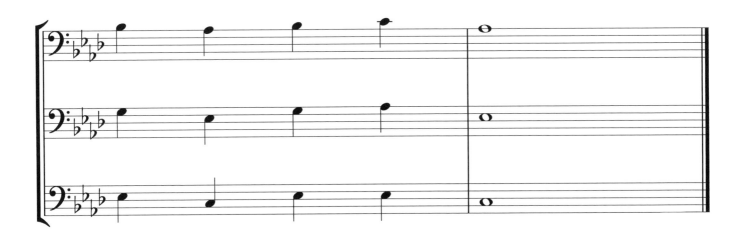

It's Raining, It's Pouring

Dreydl, Dreydl

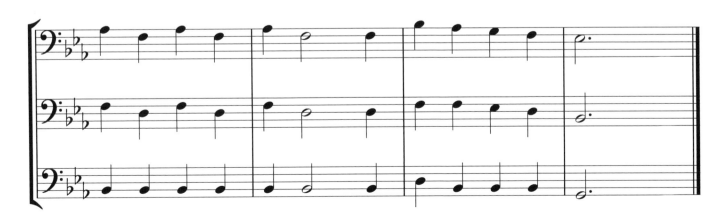

Twinkle, Twinkle, Little Star

The Victors March

Jolly Old St. Nicholas

Cassion song

The Bridge at Avignon

A Tisket, A Tasket

Barcarolle

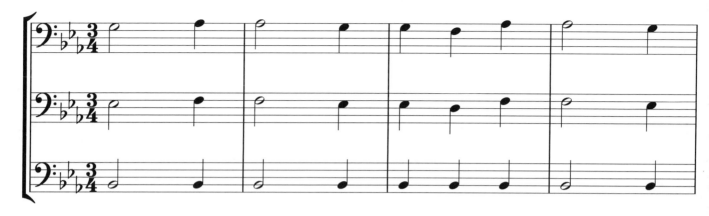

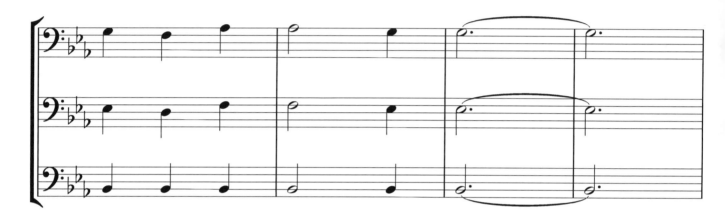

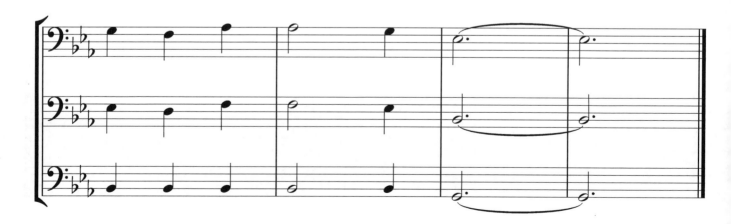

Pop Goes the Weasel

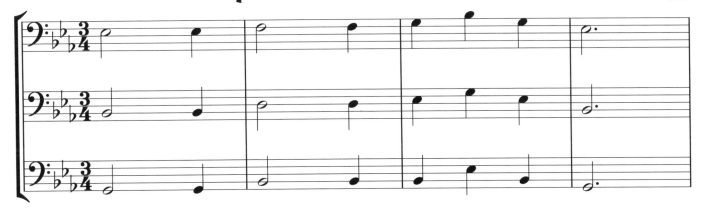

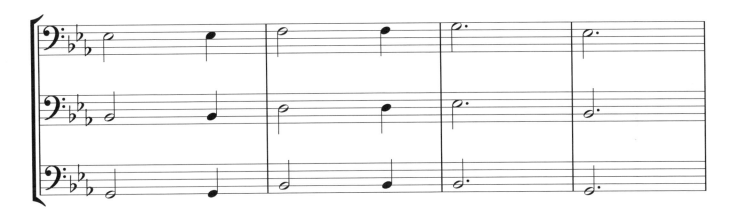

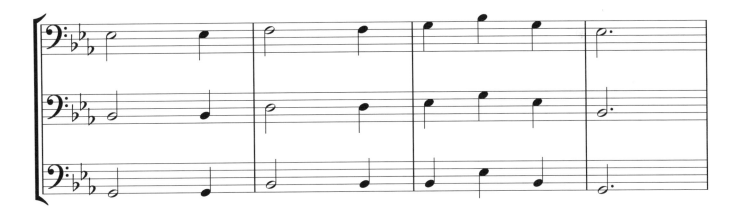

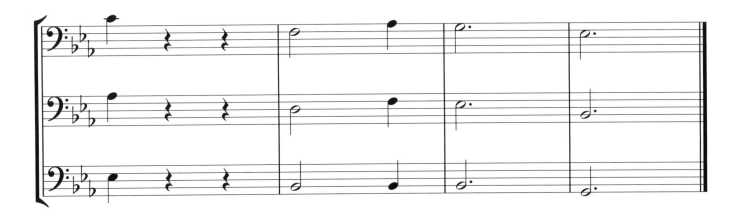

Hickory Dickory Dock

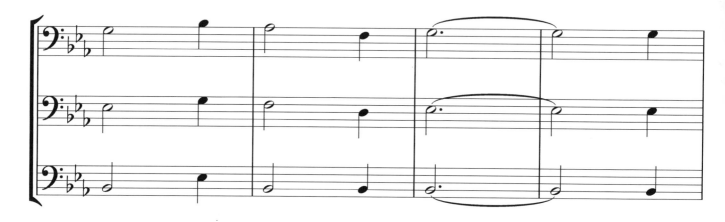

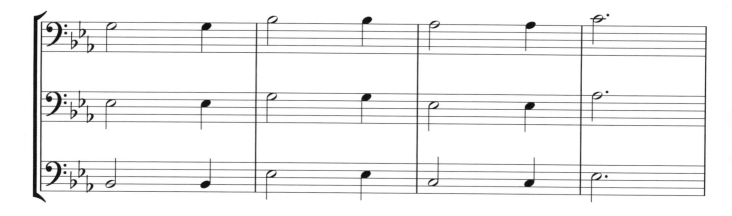

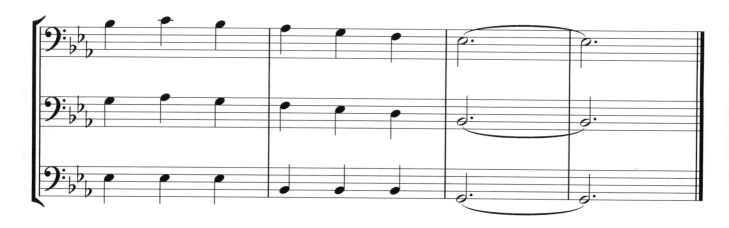

Looby Loo

Beautiful Brown Eyes

Goodbye Old Paint

Lovely Evening

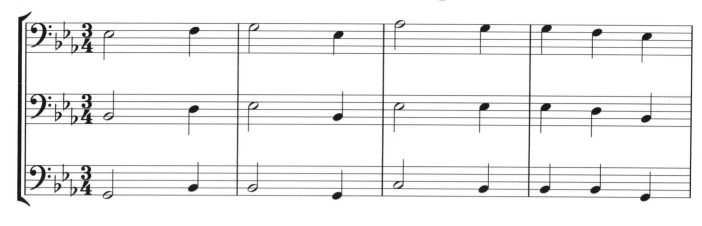

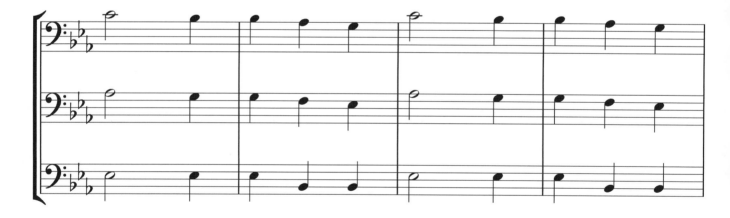

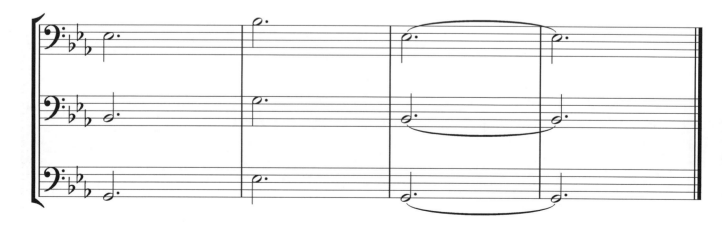

For He's a Jolly Good Fellow

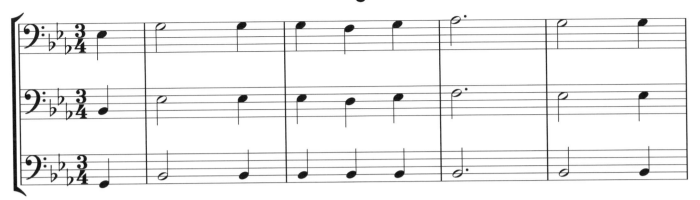

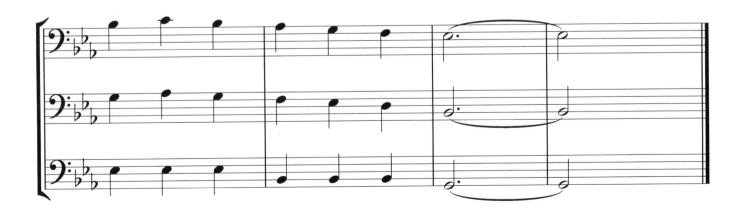

Blow the Man Down

Carnival of Venice

Morning from Peer Gynt

Lullaby

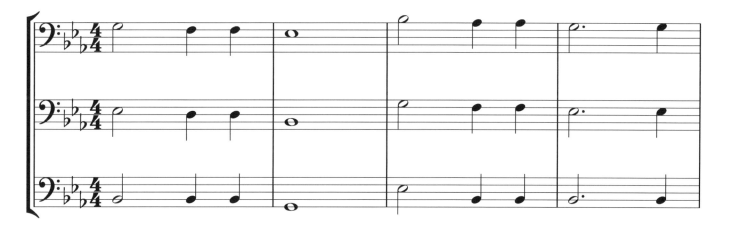

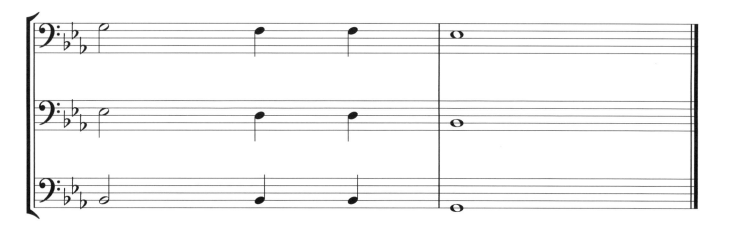

Over My Head

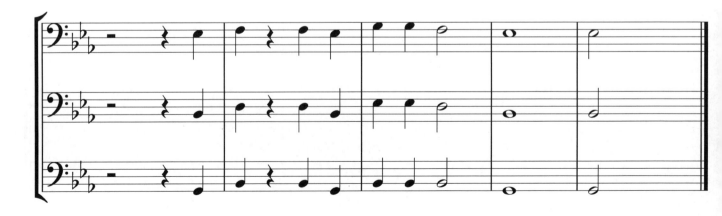

Erie Canal

Frere Jacques

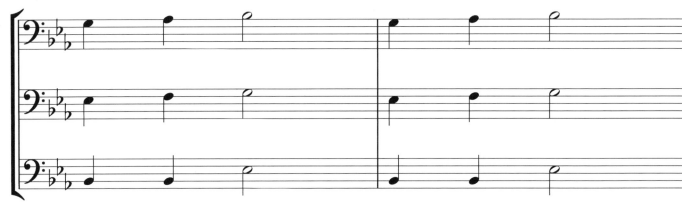

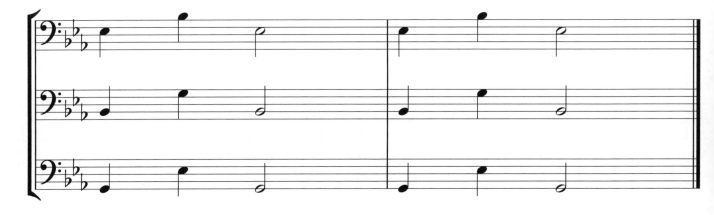

Jingle Bells

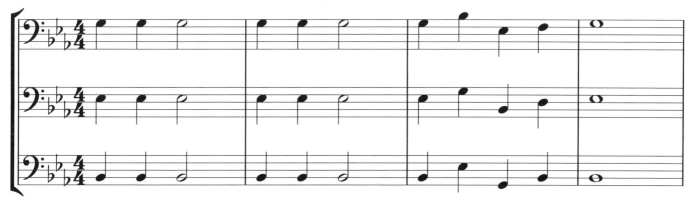

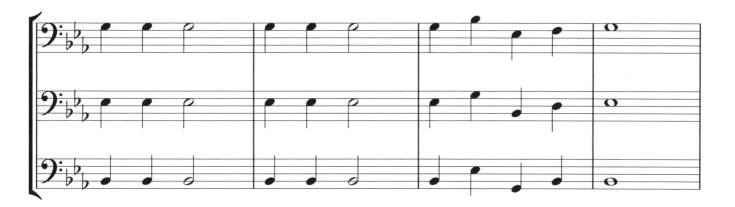

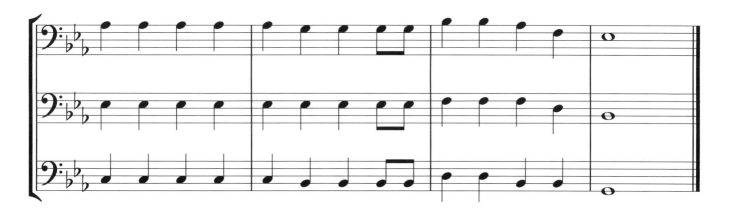

Musette

Symphony No.1 by Brahms

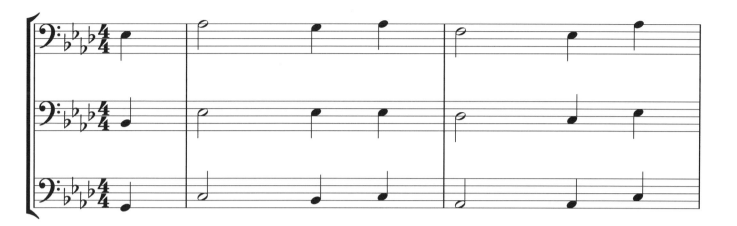

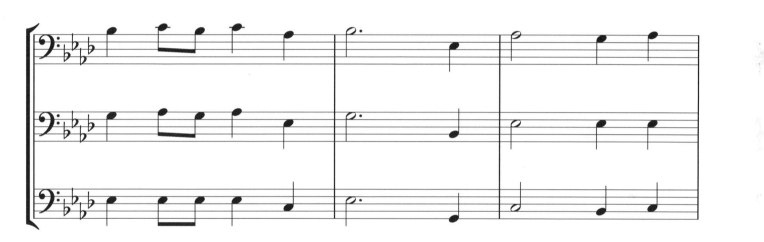

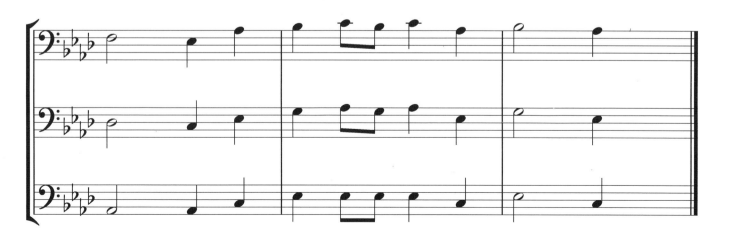

Lo Yisa Goy

Baa Baa Black sheep

This Little Light of Mine

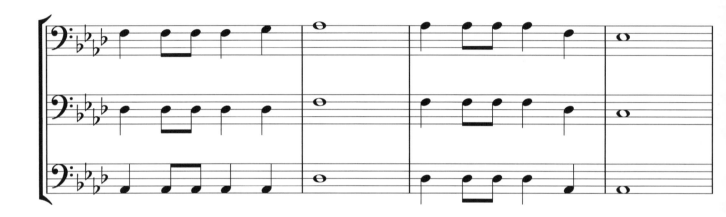

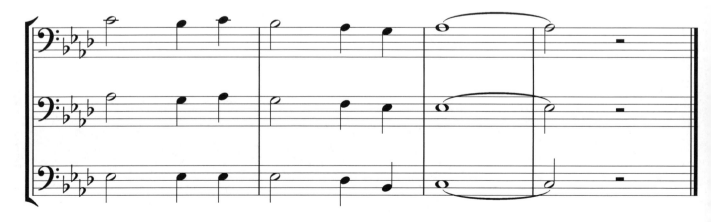

Up on the House Top

Andantino

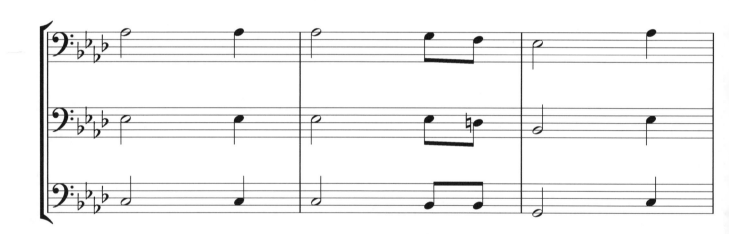

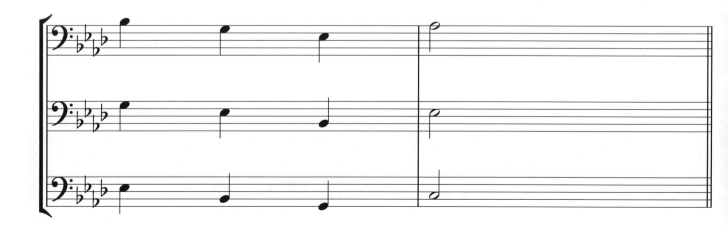

This Old Man

Bonjour, Mes Amis

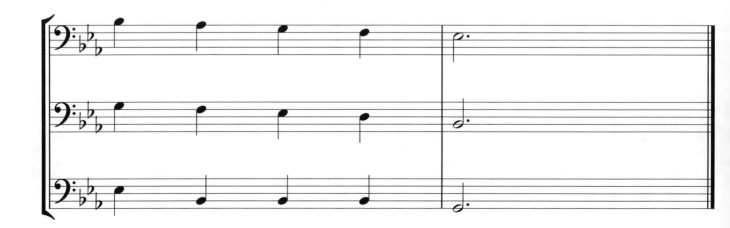

Oranges and Lemons

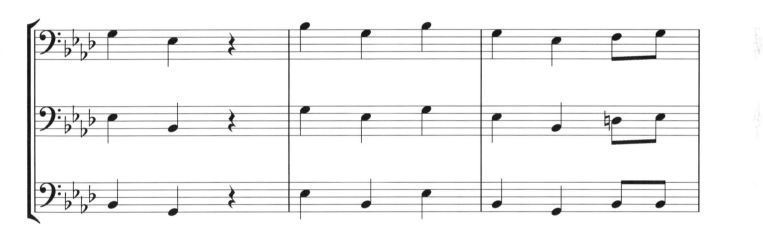

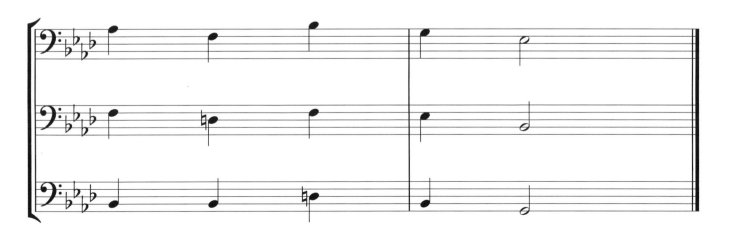

Old MacDonald

There's a Hole in the Bucket

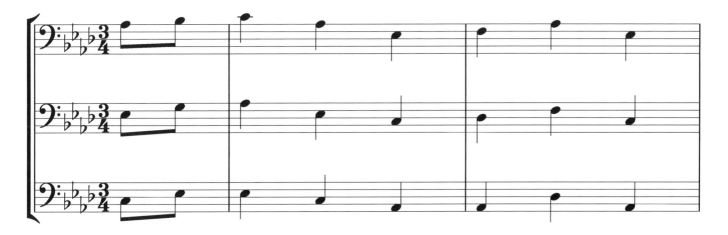

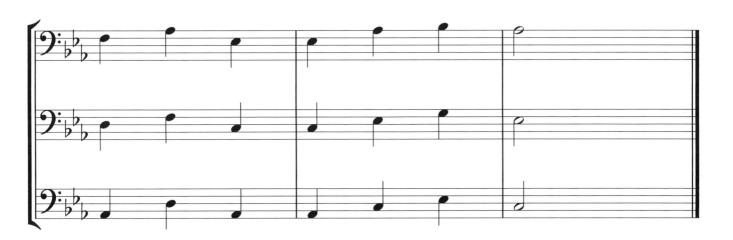

Academic Festive Overture

spring Theme from the Four seasons

El Juego Chirimbol

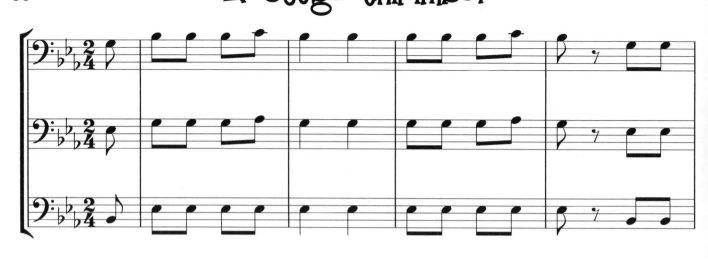

Tom Dooley

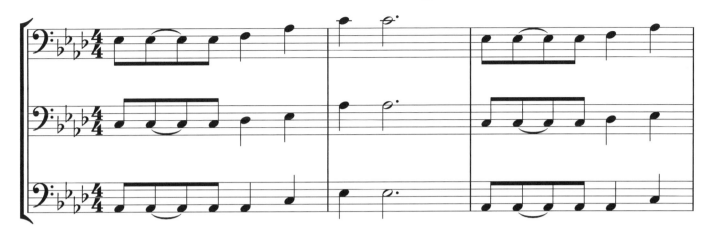

Rock·a·my·soul

Largo from New World symphony

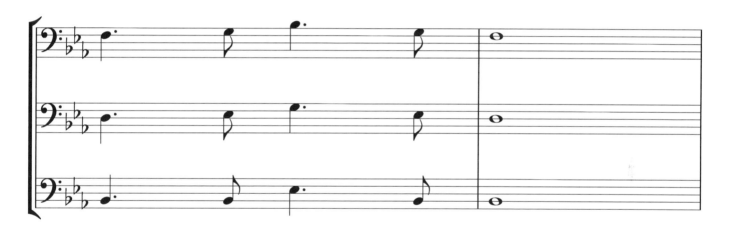

Trumpet Voluntary

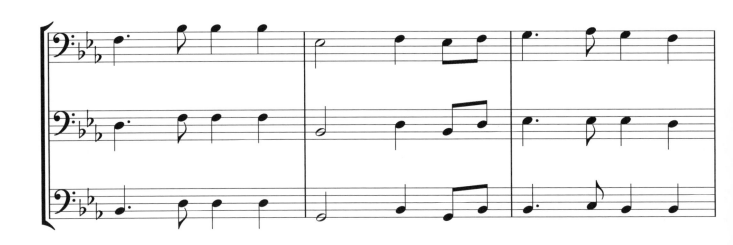

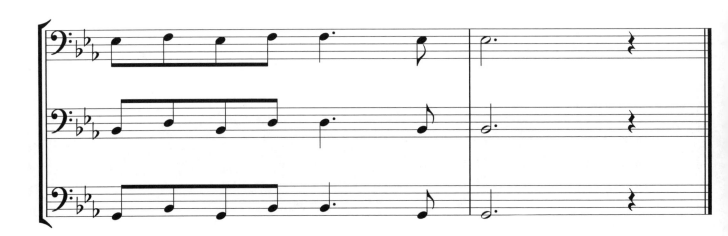

Tezna, Tezna

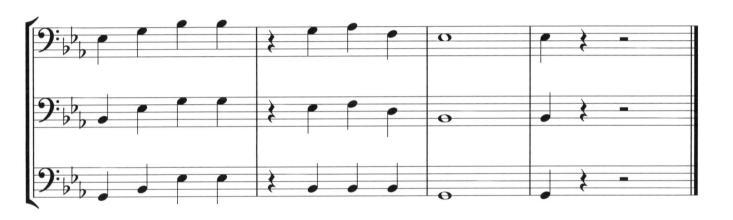

Happy Little Donkey

A New Alouette

Kum Ba Yah

Ode to Joy

Oh, susana

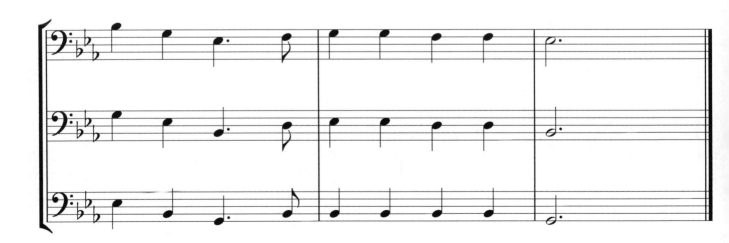

Give Me that Old Time Religion

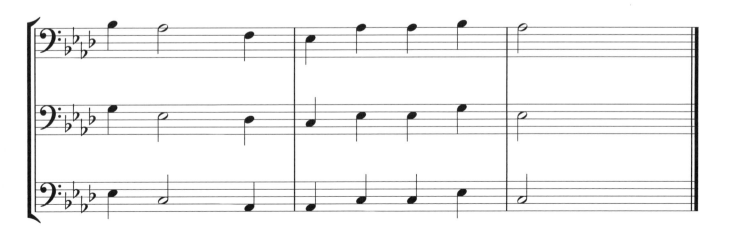

Shepherd's Hey

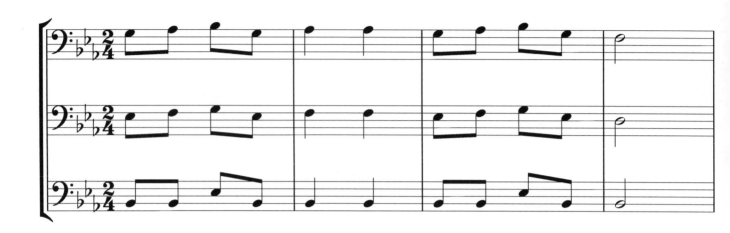

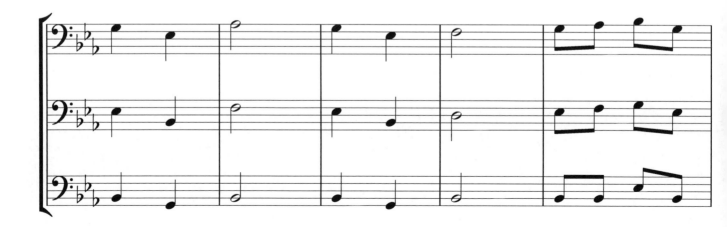

San Sereni

Printed in Great Britain
by Amazon

29070342R10040